Presented to: _____

By: _____

On: _____

Read with Me Bible

NIrV
Bible Storybook

Illustrated by
Dennis Jones

Edited by
Doris Rikkers and Jean E. Syswerda

ZONDER**kidz**

ZONDERVAN.com/
AUTHORTRACKER
follow your favorite authors

*A special thank-you to Nancy Bordewyk for the initial work
on these Bible story selections as they appeared in the New
International Version. Thanks also to Sarah Hupp for the
adaptation of the material to the New International Reader's
Version, and to Catherine DeVries for her project management
and editorial expertise on the revised and updated edition.*

Read with Me Bible, New Testament
Copyright © 2009 by Zondervan
Illustrations © 2000 by Dennis G. Jones

Requests for information should be addressed to:
Zonderkidz, Grand Rapids, Michigan 49530

ISBN: 978-0-310-61233-9

Printed in China

09 10 11 12 • 4 3 2 1

Contents

NEW TESTAMENT

Mary and the Angel

Luke 1

God sent the angel Gabriel to a virgin.
The girl was engaged to a man named
Joseph. The virgin's name was Mary.
The angel said, "The Lord is with
you." Mary was very upset. But the
angel said, "Do not be afraid, Mary.
God is pleased with you. You will give
birth to a son. You must name him
Jesus."

"How can this happen?" Mary asked. The angel answered, "The Holy Spirit will come to you. The holy one that is born will be called the Son of God. Nothing is impossible with God."

"I serve the Lord," Mary answered. "May it happen to me just as you said it would." Then the angel left her.

Jesus Is Born

Luke 2

Caesar Augustus required that a list be made of everyone in the whole Roman world. All went to their own towns to be listed.

Joseph went to Bethlehem, the town of David.
He went there with Mary. Mary was engaged to
him. She was expecting a baby.

While Joseph and Mary were there, the time
came for the child to be born. She gave birth
to her first baby. It was a boy. She wrapped
him in large strips of cloth. Then she placed
him in a manger. There was no room for
them in the inn.

The Shepherds and the Angels

Luke 2

There were shepherds living in the fields. It was night. They were looking after their sheep.

An angel of the Lord appeared to them.
The glory of the Lord shone around them.
And they were terrified.

But the angel said to them, "Do not be afraid.
I bring you good news of great joy. It is for
all the people. Today in the town of David a
Savior has been born. He is Christ the Lord.
You will find a baby wrapped in strips of cloth
and lying in a manger."

Suddenly a large group of angels appeared.
They were praising God. They said, "May glory
be given to God in heaven! And peace on earth."

The angels left and went into heaven.
The shepherds hurried off.

They found Mary and Joseph and the
baby. The baby was lying in the manger.

After the shepherds had seen him, they told
everyone. They reported what the angel had
said. All who heard it were amazed at what
the shepherds said.

Taking Jesus to the Temple
Luke 2

Joseph and Mary took Jesus to Jerusalem. They presented him to the Lord. In Jerusalem there was a man named Simeon. The Holy Spirit had told Simeon that he would not die before he had seen the Lord's Christ. The spirit led him into the temple courtyard. Then Jesus' parents brought the child in. Simeon took Jesus in his arms and praised God.

There was also a prophet named Anna. Anna was very old. She never left the temple. She worshiped night and day. Anna came up to Jesus' family. She gave thanks to God.

Joseph and Mary returned to their own town. And Jesus grew and became strong. He was very wise. He was blessed by God's grace.

The Wise Men Visit Jesus

Matthew 2

After Jesus' birth, Wise Men from the east came to Jerusalem. They asked, "Where is the child who has been born to be king of the Jews? When we were in the east, we saw his star. Now we have come to worship him."

King Herod heard about it.
He was upset.

Herod called for the Wise Men. He found out
when the star had appeared.

He sent them to Bethlehem. He said, "Make
a careful search for the child. As soon as you
find him, bring me a report. Then I can go
and worship him too."

The Wise Men went on their way. The star went ahead of them. It finally stopped over the place where the child was. When they saw the star, they were filled with joy.

The Wise Men went to the house. There they saw the child with his mother Mary. They bowed down and worshiped him. Then they opened their treasures. They gave him gold, incense and myrrh.

God warned them in a
dream not to go back to Herod.
So they returned on a different road.

32

The Escape to Egypt
Matthew 2

When the Wise Men had left, an angel appeared to Joseph in a dream. "Get up!" the angel said. "Take the child and his mother and escape to Egypt. Stay there until I tell you to come back. Herod wants to kill him."

Joseph got up. During the night, he left for Egypt with the child and his mother Mary. They stayed there until King Herod died.

The Boy Jesus at the Temple
Luke 2

Every year Jesus' parents went to Jerusalem for the Passover Feast. When he was 12 years old, they went to the Feast as usual. After the Feast was over, his parents left to go home. Jesus stayed behind in Jerusalem.

But they were not aware of it. They thought he was somewhere in their group. So they traveled on for a day. Then they began to look for him among their friends. They did not find him. So they went back to Jerusalem to look for him.

After three days they found him in the temple. He was sitting with the teachers, listening to them and asking them questions. Everyone who heard him was amazed at how much he understood. They also were amazed at his answers.

When his parents saw him, they were amazed.
His mother said, "Why have you treated us
like this? Your father and I have been worried
about you. We have been looking for you
everywhere." "Why were you looking for me?"
he asked. "Didn't you know I had to be in my
Father's house?" But they did not understand
what he meant.

Then he went back to Nazareth with them, and he obeyed them. Jesus became wiser and stronger. He became more pleasing to God and to people.

John the Baptist

Matthew 3; Mark 1

John the Baptist preached in the desert.
People went to him from all of Judea.
John baptized them in the Jordan River.

John's clothes were made of camel's hair. He had a leather belt around his waist. His food was locusts and wild honey. John said, "I baptize you with water. But after me, one will come who is more powerful than I am. I'm not fit to carry his sandals. He will baptize you with the Holy Spirit."

Jesus Is Baptized
Matthew 3

Jesus came to the
Jordan River.
He wanted to be
baptized by John.

As soon as Jesus was baptized, he came up out of the water. At that moment heaven was opened. Jesus saw the Spirit of God coming down on him like a dove. A voice from heaven said, "This is my Son, and I love him. I am very pleased with him."

Jesus Calls the Disciples

Matthew 4; Mark 2

One day Jesus was walking beside the Sea of
Galilee. He saw Simon Peter and his brother
Andrew. They were throwing a net into the
lake. They were fishermen. "Come. Follow me,"
Jesus said. "I will make you fishers of men." At
once they left their nets and followed him.

Later, Jesus saw two other brothers, James and John. They were in a boat with their father. As they were preparing their nets, Jesus called them. Right away they left the boat and their father and followed Jesus.

Once again, Jesus went out beside the sea. As he walked along he saw Levi sitting at the tax collector's booth. "Follow me," Jesus told him. Levi got up and followed him.

Jesus Changes Water to Wine

John 2

A wedding took place at Cana. Jesus' mother was there. Jesus and his disciples were also invited to the wedding.

When the wine was gone, Jesus' mother said to him, "They have no more wine." His mother said to the servants, "Do what he tells you." Six stone water jars stood nearby. Jesus said to the servants, "Fill the jars with water." So they filled them to the top.

He told them, "Now dip some out. Take it to the person in charge of the dinner." The person in charge tasted the water that had been turned into wine. He called the groom to one side. He said, "You have saved the best wine until now." That was the first of Jesus' miraculous signs.

Jesus Teaches About Praying

Matthew 5–6

Jesus went up on a mountainside and sat down.
His disciples came to him. Then he began to teach
them. He said, "This is how you should pray:

Our Father in heaven, may your name be honored.
May your kingdom come.
May what you want to happen be done on earth
     as it is done in heaven.
Give us today our daily bread.
Forgive us our sins, just as we also have forgiven
     those who sin against us.
Keep us from sin when we are tempted.
Save us from the evil one."

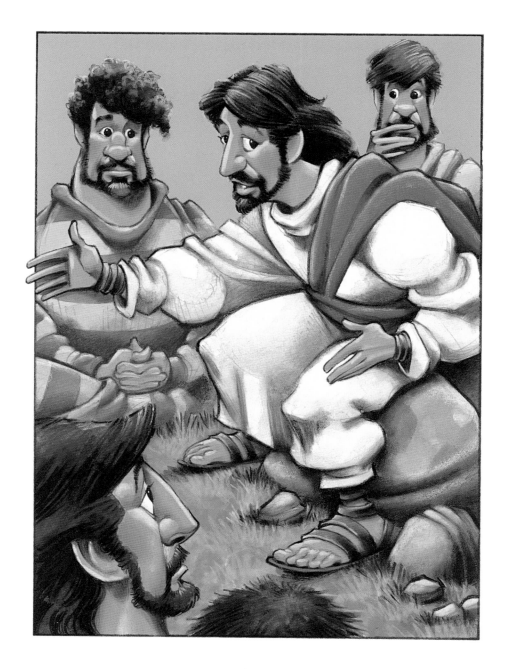

A Man Who Could Not Walk

Mark 2; Luke 5

One day Jesus was teaching. Some men came carrying a man who could not walk. But they could not get him close to Jesus because of the crowd.

They made a hole in
the roof above Jesus. Then
they lowered the man through it on a mat. They
lowered him into the middle of the crowd, right in
front of Jesus.

When Jesus saw they had faith, he said to the man who could not walk, "Get up. Take your mat and go home."

Right away, the man stood up.
He took his mat and went home praising God.
All the people were amazed. They praised God
and said, "We have never seen anything like this!"

Jesus Calms the Storm

Matthew 8; Mark 4; Luke 8

One day Jesus said to his disciples, "Let's go over to the other side of the lake."

As they sailed, a storm came on the lake.
Waves crashed over the boat. It was about to
sink. But Jesus was sleeping.

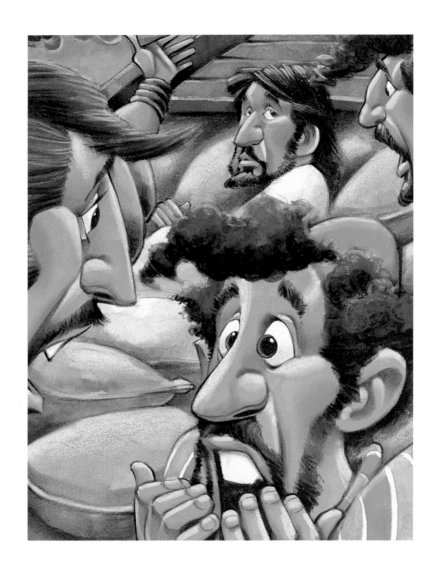

The disciples woke him up. They said,
"Don't you care if we drown?"

Jesus got up and ordered the wind and waves to stop. He said, "Quiet! Be still!" The wind died down. It was completely calm.

He said to his disciples, "Why are you so afraid? Don't you have any faith?" They were terrified. They asked each other, "Who is this? Even the wind and waves obey him!"

A Girl Who Died

Matthew 9; Mark 5

A man named Jairus came. He begged Jesus, "My daughter has just died. But come and place your hand on her. Then she will live again." Jesus went with him.

They came to Jairus' home. People were crying.
Jesus went inside. He said, "The child is not dead.
She is only sleeping." But they laughed at him.

He made them go outside. He took the child's father and mother in where the child was. He took her by the hand. He said, "Little girl, get up!"

Right away she stood up and walked around.
They were totally amazed at this.

Jesus Feeds 5,000

Matthew 14; Luke 9; John 6

Jesus saw a large crowd. He felt deep concern for them. He healed their sick people.

Late in the afternoon the disciples came to him. They said, "Send the crowd away. They can go find food. There is nothing here." Jesus replied, "They don't need to go away. You give them something to eat."

Andrew spoke up: "Here is a boy.

He has five loaves of bread. He also has two small fish. But how far will that go?"

Jesus told the people to sit on the grass.
He took the loaves and the fishes.
He gave thanks. He broke them
into pieces. He gave them to
the disciples to set in front
of the people.

When all of them had enough to eat,
Jesus said, "Gather the leftover pieces.
Don't waste anything."

The disciples picked up 12 baskets of leftover pieces. The number of men who ate was about 5,000. Women and children also ate.

Jesus Walks on Water
Matthew 14; Mark 6; John 6

Jesus made the disciples get into the boat.
He had them go ahead of him to Bethsaida.
He went up on a mountainside to pray.

When evening came, the boat was in the middle
of the lake. Jesus was alone on land. He saw the
disciples pulling hard on the oars. The wind was
blowing against them.

Jesus went out to the disciples. He walked on the lake. They saw him walking on the lake. They thought he was a ghost. They were terrified.

Right away he said, "Be brave! It is I. Don't be afraid."

"Lord, is it you?" Peter asked.
"Tell me to come to you on the water."
"Come," Jesus said. So Peter got out of the boat.

He walked on the water to Jesus. But when he saw
the wind, he was afraid. He began to sink. He cried,
"Lord! Save me!"

Right away Jesus reached out his hand and caught him. When they climbed into the boat, the wind died down. Then those in the boat worshiped Jesus. They said, "You really are the Son of God."

The Good Samaritan
Luke 10

Jesus told this story to the people:
A man was going from Jerusalem to
Jericho. Robbers attacked him.

They stripped off his clothes and
beat him. Then they went away,
leaving him almost dead.

A priest happened to be going down that same road. When he saw the man, he passed by on the other side.

A Levite passed by on the other side too.

But a Samaritan came and felt sorry for the man.
He went to him and poured olive oil and wine on
his wounds. He put the man on his own donkey,
took him to an inn and took care of him.

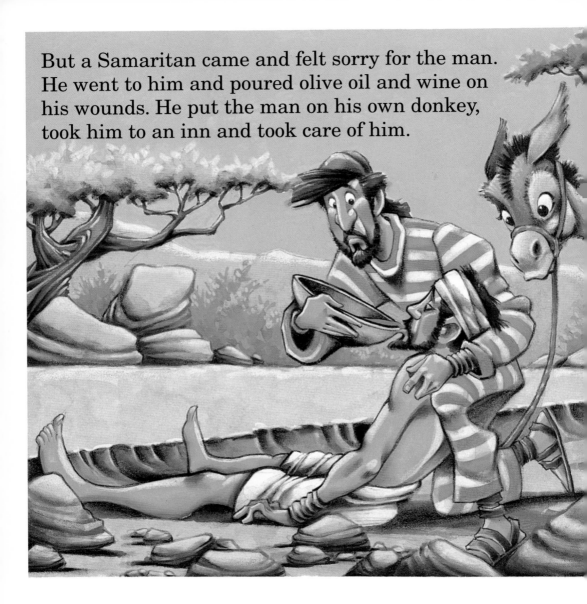

The next day he gave two silver coins to the owner of the inn. "Take care of him," he said. "When I return, I will pay you for any extra expense."

Jesus said, "Which of the three do you think was a neighbor to the man who was attacked?" The authority on the law replied, "The one who felt sorry for him." Jesus told him, "Go and do as he did."

At Mary and Martha's Home
Luke 10

Jesus came to a village where a woman named
Martha lived. She welcomed him into her home.

She had a sister named Mary. Mary sat at the Lord's feet listening to what he said.

But Martha was busy with all
the things that had to be done.

She came to Jesus and said, "My sister has left me to do the work by myself. Don't you care? Tell her to help me!"

"Martha, Martha," the Lord answered. "You are worried and upset about many things. But only one thing is needed. Mary has chosen what is better. And it will not be taken away from her."

Jesus Raises Lazarus

John 11

Mary and Martha's brother Lazarus was sick. So the sisters sent a message to Jesus. "Lord," they told him, "the one you love is sick."

Jesus loved Martha and Mary and Lazarus.
But after he heard Lazarus was sick, he
stayed where he was for two more days.
Then he said to his disciples, "Lazarus is
dead. But let us go to him."

When Jesus arrived, he found out that Lazarus
had already been in the tomb for four days. Many
Jews had come to Martha and Mary to comfort
them. "Where have you put him?" Jesus asked.
"Come and see, Lord," they replied. Jesus sobbed.
Then the Jews said, "See how much he loved him!"

Jesus came to the tomb. It was a cave with a stone in front. "Take away the stone," he said. "Lord," said Martha, "by this time there is a bad smell. Lazarus has been in the tomb for four days." Then Jesus said, "Didn't I tell you that if you believed, you would see God's glory?" So they took away the stone.

Jesus called in a loud voice, "Lazarus, come out!" The dead man came out. His hands and feet were wrapped with strips of linen. A cloth was around his face. Jesus said to them, "Take off the clothes he was buried in and let him go." Many of the Jews who had come to visit Mary saw what Jesus did. So they put their faith in him.

The Story of the Lost Sheep

Luke 15

Jesus told a story. He said:
Suppose one of you has 100 sheep and loses one of them. Won't he leave the 99 in the open country? Won't he go and look for the one lost sheep until he finds it? When he finds it, he will joyfully put it on his shoulders and go home. Then he will call his friends and neighbors.

He will say, "Be joyful with me. I have found my lost sheep." I tell you, it will be the same in heaven. There will be great joy when one sinner turns away from sin. Yes, there will be more joy than for 99 godly people who do not need to turn away from their sins.

The Story of the Lost Coin
Luke 15

Jesus told a story:
Suppose a woman has ten silver coins and loses
one. She will light a lamp and sweep the house.
She will search carefully until she finds the coin.

And when she finds it, she will call her friends and neighbors. She will say, "Be joyful with me. I have found my lost coin." I tell you, it is the same in heaven. There is joy in heaven over one sinner who turns away from sin.

The Story of the Lost Son

Luke 15

Jesus told a story:
A man had two sons. The younger son spoke to his
father. He said, "Father, give me my share of the
family property." So the father divided his property
between his two sons.

Not long after that, the younger son packed up all he had. He left for a country far away. There he wasted his money on wild living.

He spent everything he had. He went to work for someone who sent him to feed pigs. He wanted to fill his stomach with the food the pigs were eating. But no one gave him anything.

Then he began to think. He said, "How many of my father's hired workers have more than enough food! But here I am dying from hunger." So he got up and went to his father.

While the son was still a long way off, his father saw him. He was filled with tender love for his son. He ran to him. He threw his arms around him and kissed him.

The son said, "Father, I have sinned. I am no longer fit to be called your son."

But the father said to his servants, "Quick! Bring the best robe and put it on him. Put a ring on his finger and sandals on his feet. Bring the fattest calf and kill it. Let's have a big dinner. My son was dead and is alive again. He was lost. And now he is found." So they began to celebrate.

Jesus Heals Ten Men

Luke 17

As Jesus was going into a village, ten men met him. They had a skin disease. They called out, "Jesus! Master! Have pity on us!"

Jesus saw them and said, "Go. Show yourselves to the priests." While they were on their way, they were healed.

When one of them saw that he was healed, he
came back. He praised God in a loud voice. He
threw himself at Jesus' feet and thanked him.

Jesus asked, "Weren't all ten healed? Where are the other nine?" Then Jesus said to him, "Get up and go. Your faith has healed you."

Jesus and the Children

Matthew 19; Mark 10; Luke 18

Some people brought little children to Jesus. They wanted him to place his hands on the children and pray for them. The disciples told the people to stop. But Jesus asked the children to come to him. "Let the little children come to me," he said. "Don't keep them away. God's kingdom belongs to people like them." Then he took the children in his arms. He put his hands on them and blessed them.

A Very Short Man

Luke 19

Zacchaeus was a tax collector and was very rich.
He wanted to see Jesus. But he was a short man.
He could not see Jesus because of the crowd.

So Zacchaeus ran and climbed a tree. Jesus reached the spot where Zacchaeus was and said, "Zacchaeus, come down at once. I must stay at your house today." So Zacchaeus came down and welcomed him gladly.

Jesus Enters Jerusalem

Matthew 21; Mark 11; Luke 19

As they approached Jerusalem, Jesus sent out two disciples. He said, "Go to the village ahead of you. As soon as you get there, you will find a donkey's colt tied up. Untie it and bring it here. If anyone says anything to you, tell him the Lord needs it." They found a colt in the street. It was tied at a doorway. They untied it. Some people asked, "What are you doing?" They answered as Jesus had told them to. So the people let them go.

The disciples brought the colt to Jesus. They threw their coats over it and put Jesus on it. A very large crowd spread their coats on the road.

Others spread branches they had cut in the fields. The whole crowd began to praise God with joy. They shouted, "Hosanna! Blessed is the one who comes in the name of the Lord! Hosanna in the highest heaven!"

Mary Pours Perfume

John 12

A dinner was given to honor Jesus. Martha
served the food. Lazarus was among those
at the table with Jesus. Then Mary took an
expensive perfume.

She poured the perfume on Jesus' feet and wiped them with her hair. The house was filled with the sweet smell of the perfume.

Judas Iscariot didn't like what Mary did.
Judas said, "Why wasn't this perfume sold and
the money given to the poor?" He didn't say
this because he cared about the poor. He said
it because he was a thief.

"Leave her alone," Jesus replied. "The perfume was meant for the day I am buried. You will always have the poor people. But you won't always have me."

Jesus Washes the Disciples' Feet

John 13

It was just before the Passover Feast.
The evening meal was being served.
So Jesus got up from the meal. He
wrapped a towel around his waist.

He poured water into a large bowl. He began to wash his disciples' feet. He dried them with the towel that was wrapped around him.

"Do you understand what I have done for you?" he asked them. "I, your Lord and Teacher, have washed your feet. So you also should wash one another's feet. I have given you an example. You should do as I have done. Now you know these things. You will be blessed if you do them."

The Lord's Supper

Matthew 26; Mark 14

The day came to celebrate the Passover Feast. Jesus sent out two of his disciples. He told them, "Go into the city. A man carrying a jar of water will meet you. Follow him. He will show you a large upstairs room. Prepare for us to eat there."

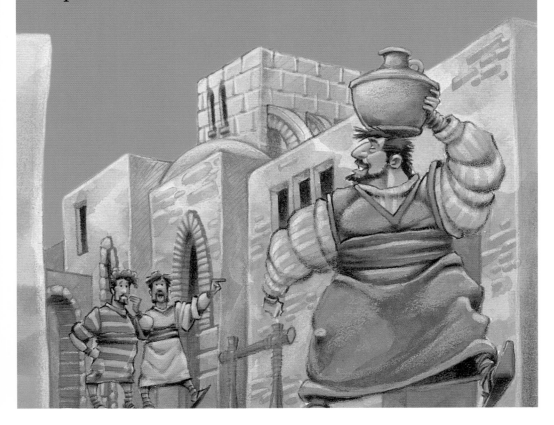

The disciples went into the city. They found things just as Jesus had told them. So they prepared the Passover meal. When evening came, Jesus arrived with the Twelve.

While they were eating, Jesus took bread. He gave thanks and broke it. He handed it to his disciples and said, "Take it. This is my body."

Then he took the cup. He gave thanks and handed it to them. All of them drank from it.

"This is my blood poured out to forgive the sins of many," he said. Then they sang a hymn and went out to the Mount of Olives.

Jesus Prays in Gethsemane

Matthew 26; Mark 14; Luke 22

Jesus and his disciples went to Gethsemane.
Jesus said, "Sit here while I pray."

He took Peter, James and John along with him. He got down on his knees and prayed, "Father, if you are willing, take this cup away from me. But do what you want, not what I want." An angel from heaven appeared to Jesus and gave him strength.

He got up from prayer and went back to the disciples. He found them sleeping. "Why are you sleeping?" he asked. "Get up! Pray that you won't fall into sin when you are tempted." Once more Jesus went away and prayed the same thing. Then he came back.

Again he found them sleeping. So he left them. For the third time he prayed. He returned to the disciples and said, "Are you still sleeping? Look! The hour is near. The Son of Man is about to be handed over to sinners. Get up! Let us go! Here comes the one who is handing me over!"

Jesus Is Arrested

Matthew 26; Mark 14; Luke 22; John 18

Jesus had finished praying. He and his disciples went into a grove of olive trees. Judas knew the place. Jesus had often been in that place. So Judas came, guiding a group of soldiers.

They were carrying torches and weapons. Jesus
asked them, "Who is it that you want?" "Jesus of
Nazareth," they replied. "I am he," Jesus said.

Judas went to Jesus. He said, "Greetings, Rabbi!" And he kissed him. Jesus asked him, "Judas, are you handing over the Son of Man with a kiss?" Peter had a sword and pulled it out. He cut off a servant's right ear. Jesus commanded Peter, "Put your sword away!" And he touched the man's ear and healed him.

Then the soldiers arrested Jesus. They tied him up.
All the disciples left and ran away.

Jesus Goes to Pilate

Matthew 27; Mark 15

Early in the morning, the priests, the elders and
the whole Sanhedrin made a decision. They tied
Jesus up. Then they handed him over to Pilate.

"Are you the king of the Jews?" asked Pilate. "Yes. It is just as you say," Jesus replied.

It was the practice at the Passover Feast to let one prisoner go free. The people could choose the one they wanted. Pilate asked, "Which one do you want me to set free? Barabbas? Or Jesus?"

"Barabbas," they answered. "What should I do with Jesus?" Pilate asked. They all answered, "Crucify him!" "Why? What wrong has he done?" asked Pilate. But they shouted even louder, "Crucify him!"

Pilate saw that he wasn't getting anywhere. So he took water and washed his hands in front of the crowd. "I am not guilty of this man's death," he said.

Pilate let Barabbas go free. But he had Jesus whipped. Then he handed him over to be nailed to a cross.

I Don't Know Him

Mark 14; Luke 22

Peter was in the courtyard. Soldiers started a fire. Then they sat down. Peter sat down with them.

A servant came by. She saw Peter. "You were with Jesus," she said. But Peter said he had not been with him. "I don't know him," he said.

A little later someone
else saw Peter. "You
are one of them,"
he said. "No," Peter
replied. "I'm not!"

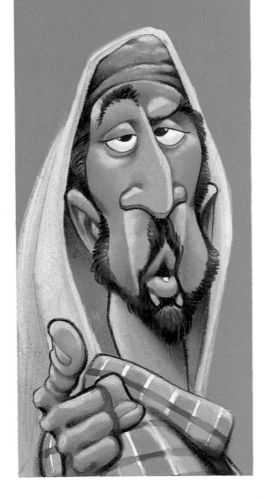

After a little while,
those standing nearby
said to Peter, "You
must be one of them."

Peter replied, "I don't know what you're talking about!" Just as he was speaking the rooster crowed.

The Lord turned and looked at Peter. Then Peter remembered what Jesus had said. "The rooster will crow. Before it does, you will say three times that you don't know me." Peter broke down and sobbed.

Jesus Dies

Matthew 27; Luke 23; John 19

Jesus had to carry his cross to a place called
The Skull. There the soldiers nailed him to
the cross.

Jesus said, "Father, forgive them. They don't know what they are doing." A written sign above him read: This is Jesus, The King of the Jews. Two robbers were crucified with him. One was on his right and one on his left. For three hours, the land was covered with darkness. Jesus cried out in a loud voice, "My God, my God, why have you deserted me?" After Jesus cried out again, he bowed his head and died.

Jesus Is Buried

Matthew 27

As evening approached, a rich man went to Pilate.
His name was Joseph. He asked for Jesus' body.
Pilate ordered that it be given to him. Joseph took
the body and wrapped it in a clean linen cloth. He
placed it in his own new tomb.

He rolled a big stone in front of the tomb. Then he went away. Pilate put a seal on the stone and placed some guards on duty.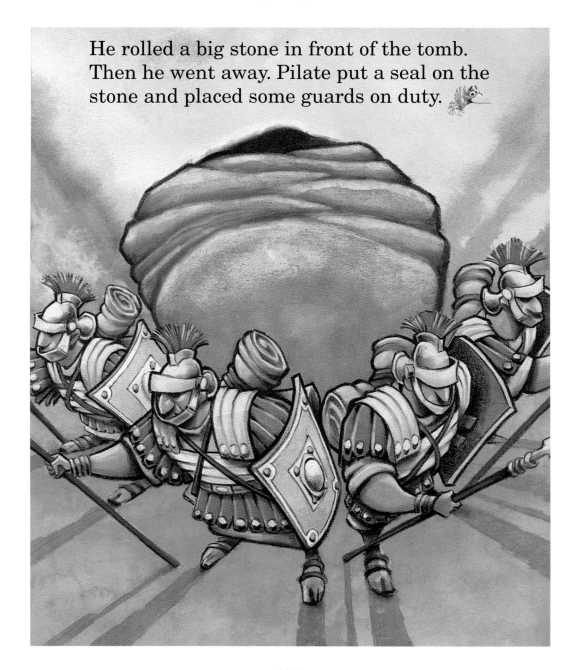

The Tomb Is Empty

Matthew 28; Mark 16; John 20

It was dawn on the first day of the week. Mary Magdalene and the other Mary went to look at the tomb. They saw that the stone had been rolled away. They entered the tomb. As they did, they saw an angel dressed in a white robe.

The angel said to the women, "Don't be afraid. I know you are looking for Jesus. He is not here! He has risen, just as he said! Go! Tell his disciples and Peter." So the women hurried away from the tomb. They were afraid, but they were filled with joy. They ran to tell the disciples.

Jesus Appears to His Disciples

Luke 24; John 20

On the evening of the first day of the week, the
disciples were together. They had locked the
doors because they were afraid of the Jews.
Jesus came in and stood among them. He said,
"May peace be with you!"

Then he showed them his hands and his side. The disciples were very happy when they saw the Lord. Jesus asked them, "Do you have anything to eat?" They gave him a piece of cooked fish. He took it and ate it in front of them.

Jesus Goes Up to Heaven

Acts 1

After his death, Jesus appeared to his disciples over a period of 40 days. After this, he was taken up to heaven. They watched until a cloud hid him from sight.

While he was going up, they kept on looking at the sky. Suddenly two men dressed in white clothing stood beside them. They said, "Why do you stand here looking at the sky? Jesus has been taken away from you into heaven. But he will come back in the same way you saw him go." So the apostles returned to Jerusalem.

The Holy Spirit Comes

Acts 2

The day of Pentecost came.
The believers all gathered in
one place. Suddenly a sound
came from heaven. It was like a
strong wind. It filled the whole
house where they were sitting.

They saw tongues of fire on each of them. They were filled with the Holy Spirit. They began to speak in languages they had not known before.

Jews from every country heard the believers speaking in their own language. The crowd was amazed. They asked, "What does this mean?" But some people made fun of the believers.

"They've had too much wine!" they said. Then Peter stood up. In a loud voice he said, "God raised Jesus back to life. We are witnesses of this. Turn away from sin and be baptized." About 3,000 people joined the believers that day.

Peter Heals a Beggar

Acts 3

One day Peter and John were going up to the temple. A man unable to walk was being carried to the temple gate called Beautiful. Every day someone put him near the gate. He would beg from people going into the temple.

He saw Peter and John. So he asked them for money. Peter looked straight at him, and so did John. Then Peter said, "Look at us! I don't have any silver or gold. But I'll give you what I have. In the name of Jesus Christ, get up and walk." Then Peter took him by the right hand and helped him up.

At once the man's feet and ankles became strong. He jumped to his feet and began to walk. He went with Peter and John into the temple. He walked and jumped and praised God. All the people were filled with wonder.

The Man from Ethiopia

Acts 8

An angel of the Lord spoke to Philip: "Go south to the desert road that goes down from Jerusalem to Gaza."

On his way he met an Ethiopian official. The man had an important position. He was in charge of all the wealth of the queen of Ethiopia. He had gone to Jerusalem to worship. On his way home he was sitting in his chariot. He was reading the book of Isaiah.

Philip heard the man reading. "Do you understand what you're reading?" Philip asked. "How can I?" he said. "I need someone to explain it." He invited Philip to come up and sit with him. Then Philip told him the good news about Jesus.

As they traveled along the road, they came to some water. The official said, "Look! Here is water! Why shouldn't I be baptized?" Then both Philip and the official went down into the water. Philip baptized him.

Saul Believes

Acts 9

Saul wanted to find men and women who
belonged to Jesus. He wanted to take them
as prisoners to Jerusalem.

On his journey, Saul approached Damascus.
Suddenly a light from heaven flashed around him.
He fell to the ground. He heard a voice say to him,
"Saul! Saul! Why are you opposing me?"
"Who are you, Lord?" Saul asked.

"I am Jesus," he replied. "I am the one you are opposing. Now get up and go into the city. There you will be told what you must do." The men traveling with Saul weren't able to speak. They heard the sound. But they didn't see anyone.

Saul got up from the ground. He opened his eyes, but he couldn't see. So the men led him by the hand into Damascus. For three days he was blind.

In Damascus there was a believer named Ananias. The Lord called to him in a vision, "Ananias! Go to the house of Judas on Straight Street. Ask for a man named Saul. He is praying."

Then Ananias went to the house.
He placed his hands on Saul.
"Brother Saul," he said, "you saw
Jesus. He has sent me so that you
will be able to see again. You will be
filled with the Holy Spirit."

Right away something like scales fell from Saul's eyes. And he could see again. He got up and was baptized.

Saul in Damascus

Acts 9

Saul spent several days with the believers in Damascus. He began to preach that Jesus is the Son of God. All who heard him were amazed. They asked, "Isn't he the man who caused great trouble in Jerusalem for those who worship Jesus?" After many days, the Jews planned to kill Saul. But he learned of their plan. Day and night they watched the city gates closely in order to kill him.

But his followers helped him escape by night. They lowered him in a basket through an opening in the wall.

Paul and Silas in Prison

Acts 13; 16

Some men in Philippi grabbed Saul, who was also known as Paul, and Silas. Paul and Silas were thrown into prison. The jailer was commanded to guard them carefully.

He put them deep inside the prison. He fastened their feet so they couldn't get away. About midnight Paul and Silas were praying and singing to God. The prisoners were listening to them.

Suddenly there was a powerful earthquake.
It shook the prison from the top to bottom. All
the prison doors flew open. Everybody's chains
came loose.

The jailer woke up. He saw the prison
doors were open. He pulled out his sword
to kill himself. He thought the prisoners
had escaped. "Don't harm yourself!" Paul
shouted. "We're all here!"

The jailer rushed in, shaking with fear. He fell down in front of Paul and Silas. Then he brought them out. He asked, "Sirs, what must I do to be saved?" They replied, "Believe in the Lord Jesus. Then you and your family will be saved."

Right away he and all his family were baptized.
The jailer brought Paul and Silas into his house.
He set a meal in front of them. He and his whole
family were filled with joy. They had become
believers in God.

Paul Sails for Rome

Acts 27

Paul and some other prisoners were put on board a
ship sailing for Rome. Before very long, the ship was
caught by a storm. It had the force of a hurricane.

The men tied ropes under the ship to hold it together. They were afraid it would get stuck on sandbars. They lowered the sea anchor and let the ship be driven along.

The storm was terrible. On the 14th night the sailors had a feeling that they were approaching land. They were afraid the ship would crash against the rocks. They dropped four anchors from the back of the ship. They prayed that daylight would come.

Just before dawn Paul tried to get them to eat. "For the last 14 days," he said, "you have gone without food. I am asking you to eat some food. You need it to live. Not one of you will lose a single hair from your head." All of them were filled with hope. So they ate.

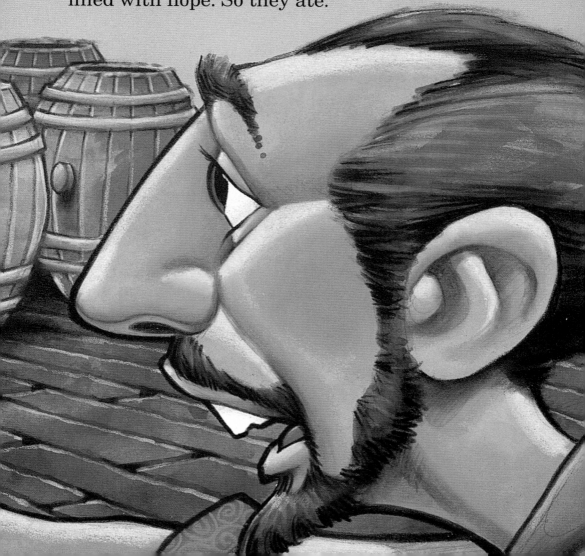

When daylight came, they saw a sandy beach.
They decided to run the ship onto the beach.
But the ship hit a sandbar and wouldn't move.

The commander ordered those who could swim to jump overboard and swim to land. The rest were supposed to get there on pieces of the ship. That is how everyone reached land safely.

Jesus Is Coming

Revelation 21–22

I heard a loud voice. It said, "Now God makes his home with human beings. He will live with them. They will be his people. And God himself will be with them and be their God.

He will wipe away every tear from their eyes. There will be no more death or crying or pain." The Lord said, "Look! I am coming soon! Blessed is anyone who obeys the words of this book. Look! I am coming soon! I am the First and the Last. I am the Beginning and the End. Yes. I am coming soon."

 # Index

You may want to read about a Bible person or event or about a lesson to be learned. This list will help you find the right story.

Words You Should Know

If you are unsure of the meaning of a word used in this book, look it up here.

A

Anchor—Something heavy, tied to a rope, which is attached to a boat. When an anchor is thrown into the water, it keeps the boat from floating away.

Angel—A spirit who is God's helper and tells people God's words.

Apostle—One of the twelve men who was with Jesus and later taught others about him.

B

Baptize—To pour on or cover a person with water as a sign that sin is washed away.

C

Caesar—The Roman king or emperor.

Chariot—A two-wheeled cart pulled by horses.

Christ—A Greek word that means *the Anointed One*. It means the same thing as the Hebrew word *Messiah*. It is part of Jesus' name.

Crucify—To put a person to death by nailing him or her to a cross.

D

Desert—Very dry and dusty land.

Disciples—the twelve men who were with Jesus and later taught others about him.

G

Glory—Praise. Honor. Greatness.

God—The Creator and Ruler of the world. The One who saves his people.

Grace—God's kindness to people. It is given without being earned.

Groom—A man who is getting married.

H

Heaven—God's home.

Herod—One of the rulers of Israel.

Holy Spirit—God's Spirit who lives in the hearts of believers and works in their lives. Jesus promised to send the Holy Spirit so that you would never be alone.

Hosanna—A Hebrew word of praise that means *please save us now.*

Hymn—A song of praise to God.

J

Jews—Another name for the people of Israel.

K

Kingdom—An area or group of people ruled by a king.

L

Language—The words that a group of people in a country speak.

Laws—Rules about what is right and wrong.

Locust—A type of grasshopper that eats and destroys crops.

Lord—A title for God that shows respect.

M

Manger—A food box for animals.

Miracle—Something that is very wonderful that only God can do, such as making a blind person see or making a crippled person walk.

Myrrh—A very sweet perfume.

P

Passover—A feast that is celebrated every springtime to remember the time when God set the people of Israel free from Egypt. God "passed over" their homes if the doorways were marked with blood.

Pentecost—A feast that is celebrated 50 days after Passover. On the day of Pentecost the Holy Spirit came just as Jesus promised.

Priest—A person who served in the temple. He gave offerings and prayers to God.

Property—Land that someone owns.

R

Rabbi—A teacher of Jewish law.

S

Samaritans—People who lived near the Jews. The Jews did not like them.

Sandbar—Hills of sand that hide under the water of a lake or ocean. Sometimes boats get stuck on sandbars and cannot float.

Sanhedrin—The most important Jewish court of law in Jesus' time.

Saved—Set free from danger or sin.

Savior—The One who sets us free from our sins. See also Jesus.

Servant—Someone who is paid to do work for you or to cook for you.

Shepherd—A person who takes care of sheep.

Sinner—A person who does things God does not like.

T

Temple—A building where people worship.

Tempt—To try to get someone to do something wrong.

Tomb—A place where a dead body is placed. It was usually a cave with a big stone door.

Twelve, the—The men Jesus chose as his first disciples. See also Disciples.

V

Virgin—A woman who has never slept with a man.

Vision—Something that God puts in a person's mind. Something like a dream, but the person is usually awake.

W

Wise Men—The three kings who came to see Jesus.

Worship—To love and praise God.